# TALKING ABOUT
# Eating and Health

## Sarah Levete

# Franklin Watts
# London • Sydney

Paperback edition published
in 2006.

© Aladdin Books Ltd 2004

Designed and produced by
Aladdin Books Ltd
2/3 Fitzroy Mews
London W1T 6DF

First published in Great Britain
in 2004 by
Franklin Watts
338 Euston Road
London NW1 3BH

Franklin Watts Australia
Hachette Children's Books
Level 17/207 Kent Street
Sydney NSW 2000

ISBN: 978-0-7496-7009-2

Design: Flick, Book Design
and Graphics
Picture research:
Brian Hunter Smart
Editors: Jim Pipe & Rebecca Pash
The consultant, Steve Bloomfield, is
Media Information Manager for the
UK Eating Disorders Association.

# Contents

# "What is healthy eating?"

What did you have for breakfast today – toast and honey, or a packet of crisps? Do you think you ate enough? Do you think it was good for your health?

During the day, you use up lots of energy. Your brain is busy learning new things, and your body is working hard, running around and playing.

To do these things you need to be in tip-top condition, and the best place to start is with a healthy "diet".

Food can be healthy and tasty, too!

Your diet is made up of the different foods that you eat. For a healthy body, it is important to eat a balanced diet that includes the right amount and types of food. Eating too little, too much or the wrong kinds of food can cause problems.

This book talks about how eating affects your mind and body. It can help you to make simple choices about food that will keep you feeling healthy and full of energy.

What you eat affects your health, whatever your age.

# "Why is healthy eating important?"

Healthy eating helps people, young and old, to stay fit and fight off illness. As you grow, your body works incredibly hard and needs a great deal of energy to do so.

Your bones are growing and your organs are developing. At this time, it is very important to eat healthy foods that contain plenty of goodness, found in substances called "nutrients".

Eating healthy foods gives your body the goodness it needs to grow. They give you energy, too!

Different foods provide the nutrients that the body needs. Without these, the body suffers. For instance, vitamin D found in fish, such as tuna, salmon or mackerel, helps bones to grow strong.

You need the iron from foods such as spinach, dried fruit, red meat and beans to keep your blood healthy.

# Did you know...

You need plenty of liquid, as well as food. The best drink is free – water. It's important to drink water or fruit juice throughout the day, especially after playing sport. Try to avoid sweet or fizzy drinks. They are full of sugar which rots your teeth. They give your body energy, but this energy may be stored as fat unless it is used up.

# "What do different foods do?"

Different foods are good for you in different ways. Fruits and vegetables, such as bananas, potatoes and carrots, contain vitamins and minerals. These are chemicals that keep your body working.

For instance, vitamin C keeps skin looking healthy and helps fight off coughs and colds. Fruits and vegetables also contain fibre to help you digest food and feel fuller for longer.

A balanced meal will contain carbohydrates, protein, fibre, and vitamins and minerals.

# Think about it

Too much fat can lead to health problems, but your body does need some fat.

Some fats are healthier than others. The fat found in foods such as burgers, crisps or ice-cream will give you a burst of energy but none of the nutrients your body needs. The fats found in sunflower or olive oil, or in nuts and oily fish, are far healthier.

Bread, pasta, potatoes and grains, such as rice and couscous, are packed with carbohydrates. These give you energy to run around and be active. Meat, fish, eggs, nuts, beans and lentils are rich in proteins. Proteins help your body to grow, repair itself and fight off illness. They help keep your hair shiny and skin healthy. Dairy foods, such as milk and cheese, contain fat and the mineral calcium which helps grow strong bones.

# "How can I eat healthily?"

You'll have more energy if you eat regular meals. The most important is breakfast. It sets you up for the rest of the day. Some cereals contain a lot of sugar. Juice, brown toast and a banana is healthier and better for your teeth. Choose fresh foods instead of ready-made foods that are packed with sugar, salt and fat. Try not to put fatty sauces such as mayonnaise all over your food. Too much salt and fat can lead to heart problems.

Try to eat a varied diet of carbohydrates, fruit and vegetables, protein-packed meat, fish, beans or nuts and dairy products.

For packed lunch at school, try pasta or couscous salad with tuna or lentils. Choose brown or wholemeal bread or pasta. It will keep you feeling full for longer.

Yoghurt or fresh fruit for pudding is tasty and healthy, too. Dried fruit, muesli bars, or sandwiches make healthy and energising snacks between meals.

# Did you know...

This food pyramid shows the different food groups.

**Fats, oils, sugars**
Crisps, cakes and sweets

**Proteins**
Meat, fish, eggs, nuts, beans

**Dairy foods**
Milk, cheese, yoghurt

**Fruit and Vegetables**

**Grains**
Rice, pasta, bread

For a healthy and balanced diet, aim to eat plenty of the foods at the bottom and only a few at the very top!

# "What if I can't eat some foods?"

All over the world, people from different cultures and countries eat different foods. Some religions do not allow certain foods. For instance, Hindus do not eat beef.

Vegetarians choose not to eat meat or fish, and vegans also avoid dairy foods such as milk. If you don't eat from one of the main food groups (page 11), make sure you get enough of the missing nutrients from other foods.

There may be religious, health or taste reasons why a person doesn't eat certain foods.

We need to eat to live, but the choices we make about food may be affected by taste or availability.

Some people dislike the taste or feel of certain foods. There is no point in having porridge for breakfast if you can't stand it! There are lots of healthy alternatives.

If you argue at home about what you eat, discuss it calmly with your parents or carers. Try to agree on what will provide a balanced and healthy diet. Decide which foods are only allowed as a treat or on special occasions.

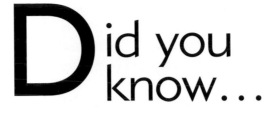

id you know…

Some people are allergic to certain foods and become unwell if they eat them. They may come out in a rash or swellings. It's important to tell someone if you have a severe allergy to any food, such as nuts.

# "What about eating and weight?"

Everyone has a different body shape. Some people are naturally thin and others are larger. But if a person eats too many fatty, sugary foods on a regular basis, he or she will gain weight. And without enough food, the body stops working properly, making a person pale, tired and unwell.

Whatever your body shape or size, healthy eating and regular exercise will help keep you fit and well.

The energy in food is measured in calories. Too few or too many calories will, over time, lead to either weight loss or weight gain.

Many grown-ups go on "slimming diets" to lose weight. These diets often fail because the person doesn't eat enough of what the body needs, feels hungry and then gives up the diet.

A child should not need to go on a "slimming diet" if he or she combines a reasonable amount of exercise with a varied, balanced diet.

# Think about it

In poor, less developed countries many people do not have enough food. The weather is often hot and dry making it difficult to grow crops or keep animals.

Young children and babies suffer from "malnutrition" as their bodies are starved of the nutrients they need. They become very underweight and may even die.

# "Why are some people overweight?"

If a person eats too many fatty, sugary foods, he or she will put on weight. A medical condition might cause some people to be overweight.

Many children today eat too many fatty, sugary foods and don't take enough exercise. They risk developing health problems such as heart disease or diabetes. To avoid this, you can make simple, healthy choices about the food you eat.

Too many fatty foods and too little exercise can damage your body.

Many people who are overweight feel unhappy about themselves and are embarrassed to join in with activities. This makes it even harder to keep fit.

Fatty, sugary foods, such as doughnuts, sweets or crisps, are tasty but that's about it! They are packed with calories but don't give the body the nutrients it needs.

Taking some regular exercise is the best way to make sure that the calories you eat are used up by your body, rather than stored as fat.

# My story

"My dad used to be overweight. He was always eating crisps, and drank lots of beer. When he played football, he'd get really out of breath. Then he had to stay in hospital. The doctors said he must lose weight or he would become ill again. Now, he eats really healthily and catches us easily when we play chase!"
Mary

# "How does eating affect the way I feel?"

Everywhere you look there are images of fit and slim men and women. Pictures in magazines and in adverts show a slim, "ideal" body shape. But in reality, people are all shapes and sizes. Many people feel pressure to look a certain way. But this can make them unhappy and may even lead to eating disorders.

Exercise and spending time with friends or family is fun and can make you feel good about yourself.

# Think about it

It is important to feel good about yourself. Spending time with friends and family can help. But, if you have a balanced diet and exercise regularly, you are likely to feel good, inside and out, whatever your shape or size.

If you do worry about your body and feel unhappy about eating, talk to a parent or someone you trust.

Pop stars or sports stars often appear in adverts for different snack foods. The stars may look great but they probably don't eat the foods they are advertising. These foods are often fatty, salty and very unhealthy.

When you look at magazine photos or adverts, remember that lots of them are adjusted to make the models look slimmer than they really are.

# "What is an eating disorder?"

An increasing number of people suffer from eating disorders. These illnesses can cause a great deal of physical harm and emotional upset.

An eating disorder is not a diet. It is not being fussy about food or having food allergies. Just because a person is thin or overweight, though, doesn't mean he or she has an eating disorder.

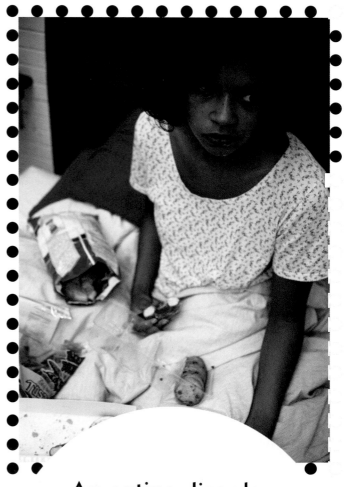

An eating disorder is a way of coping with other difficult feelings.

When a person has an eating disorder, his or her eating is out of control. He or she either eats far too much, or hardly eats at all.

The person uses food as a way to cope with other problems, such as difficulties at home or school, or anxiety about his or her looks.

An eating disorder can affect boys or girls at any time. Sufferers will constantly think about food, their image and their weight. It takes over their lives.

# Think about it

Many people have anxieties about body image and weight. But a person with an eating disorder may:

• have a constant anxiety and worry about food

• always be thinking about their body image and weight

• try to avoid meal times

• be secretive about eating

• exercise excessively

• feel guilty about eating

# "What is anorexia nervosa?"

A person with the eating disorder anorexia nervosa may think that they are fat, despite eating very little and becoming very underweight.

He or she often exercises excessively, works out the calories in every tiny piece of food and avoids social situations involving food.

Starving the body is a way of blocking out another problem. Stress at school or feeling unhappy can trigger the start of anorexia.

A person with anorexia nervosa will go to great lengths to avoid eating.

People with anorexia and other eating disorders often feel that eating is the one thing over which they have control. But in fact, their behaviour is out of control and is so obsessive that it takes over their lives.

# My story

"My sister was always worried about her exams. Then she started to get really thin. She'd pretend she'd already eaten and even worry about eating an apple. She kept fainting and had to go to hospital. Now she sees a counsellor which has helped her to talk about her difficulties with eating. It has really helped and she's slowly getting better." Julie

Anorexia is a dangerous illness. As well as losing a lot of weight, a person may feel dizzy and cold, have dry skin, grow extra body hair, and, in girls, periods may stop. It can lead to heart failure, and even death.

# "What is bulimia nervosa?"

A person with the eating disorder bulimia nervosa eats large amounts, known as binging. He or she is then deliberately sick to get rid of the food. The effect of being sick can cause tooth decay, stomach problems and even heart failure. A person with bulimia may also exercise excessively to use up the calories from any food. He or she may feel tired and have severe mood swings.

A person with bulimia often feels ashamed but is unable to control his or her eating.

Bulimia is often unnoticed as sufferers may not be obviously very thin, or very overweight. A person with bulimia may find it hard to admit to the problem and seek help because of the intense feelings of shame.

Like anorexia, bulimia is a way of blocking out other difficulties. It causes great physical and emotional distress, and a sufferer needs help from a professional, such as a counsellor, in order to recover.

# Did you know...

Some people eat large amounts over a long period of time. They eat to block out other feelings. They feel guilty and want to lose weight, but the food distracts them from the real problem.

This is called compulsive eating, and like other eating disorders, sufferers need special help to get better.

# "How do you recover from eating disorders?"

There is no quick fix to an eating disorder. It takes time and patience. The first step is to tell another person. People often don't want to do this because they feel ashamed and guilty. They may find it hard to admit that they have a problem. But confiding in someone, such as a parent or teacher, is an important first step.

Talking helps a person understand what lies behind the eating disorder and what may have "triggered" it.

Getting better is not just a question of "eating up". For someone with an eating disorder, eating regular amounts feels impossible.

A counsellor can help the person take the first steps towards a regular eating pattern by uncovering the difficulties and feelings behind the eating disorder.

In some cases, people need to spend some time in hospital. But with time and support, most people recover.

# Did you know...

An eating disorder doesn't just affect the sufferer. It is really hard for parents, brothers and sisters and friends, too.

The understanding and support from family and friends is very important as a person gets over an eating disorder. If you know someone who you think has an eating disorder, encourage him or her to tell a grown-up.

# "How can food be fun?"

Food is an important and fun part of many cultures. Special foods are prepared for festivals and celebrations. A birthday party wouldn't be the same without a cake!

Remember, we need to eat to live, so it helps to enjoy food. Don't feel guilty about eating a treat now and then.

Having a balanced diet doesn't mean going without treats. It just means being aware that you are choosing foods that give your body what it needs.

Enjoy treats.
Enjoy eating and feeling well.

Good food is easy and fun to prepare. Ask your parents or carers if you can help cook a meal. Try experimenting – you may discover a tasty new recipe!

Why not ask your parents or carers if you can help with the shopping. Choose plenty of healthy, tasty foods and a few delicious treats, too!

# Did you know...

Keeping healthy is not just about what you eat. Good hygiene is very important, too. This includes washing hands with warm, soapy water before cooking or eating to get rid of any bugs that could give you an upset stomach.

Tiny bits of food can get caught between teeth and cause decay, so remember to brush your teeth. It's especially important to clean your teeth after sugary foods and sweet, fizzy drinks.

# "What can I do?"

- To stay fit and enjoy your food, eat regular meals and a wide variety of food.
- Eat plenty of fruit and vegetables, and choose brown bread or pasta.
- Drink plenty of water.
- Cut back on too many fatty, sugary and salty foods.
- Brush your teeth regularly.
- Take some regular, moderate exercise.
- Join in activities that you enjoy and that make you feel good about yourself.
- Everyone, including you, has a unique shape and look – be proud of yourself!
- Talk to a grown-up about any concerns you have.

To stay fighting fit, eat well, enjoy your food and keep active.

# Books on eating & health

If you want to read more, try:

*Let's Discuss Anorexia & Bulimia*
by Pete Sanders & Steve Myers
(Franklin Watts)
*My Healthy Body: Digestion*
by Jen Green (Franklin Watts)

# Contact information

If you want to talk to someone who doesn't know you, these organisations can help:

British Nutrition Foundation
High Holborn House, 52-54 High Holborn,
London WC1V 6RQ
Tel: 020 7404 6504
Promotes nutritional wellbeing of society.

Eating Disorder Association
103 Prince of Wales Rd, Norwich, NR1 1DW
Youth helpline: 0845 6347650
Email: feedback@edauk.com
Offers advice, information and support.

Childline
Tel: 0800 1111
A 24-hour free helpline for children.

# On the web

These websites are also helpful:

www.nutrition.org.uk
www.childrenfirst.nhs.uk
www.eduak.com
www.freshforkids.com.au
www.activekidz.com.au
www.reachout.com.au

Kids Helpline,
Australia
Tel: 1800 55 1800
A 24-hour free
helpline for children.

Nutrition Australia
6/100 Campbell Street,
Queensland 4006
Tel: 073 257 4393
Offices throughout the
country offer advice and
information on health and nutrition.

Eating Disorders Foundation
1513 High Street, Glen Iris, Victoria 3146
Tel: 1300 550 236
Offers support and advice to those whose lives are affected by eating disorders.

**There is lots of useful information about eating and health on the internet.**

# Index

## Photocredits

Abbreviations: l-left, r-right, b-bottom, t-top, c-centre, m-middle
Front cover, 20r, 23br, 25br — Photodisc. 1, 17br, 29b, 30b — Digital Vision. 2, 6r, 19tl, 21br, 22r — Brand X
Pictures. 3tr, 9tl, 27br — Image 100. 3mr, 4r, 10br, 12r — Ken Hammond/USDA. 3br, 16r, 18b, 28r —
Corbis. 5b, 7b, 13r — Jim Pipe. 8br, 14br, 15br, 19r — Corel. 11 all Stockbyte except for milk — Brand X
Pictures, and rice — Keith Weller/USDA. 13br — Stockbyte. 24b, 26br — PBD.